My Story is dedicated to all the shelter dogs out there who haven't been adopted and the humans that work tirelessly everyday to find them homes and save them.

Don't give up. We are worth saving.

The Animal Care Center in St John, US Virgin Islands. A No-Kill shelter dedicated to saving the lives of the islands' homeless and neglected animals.

I am Moose.

I was brought to the Animal Care Center (ACC) in February 2011 when I was found running with the head of a pack of 1000 runners getting ready for the Islands' annual '8 Tuff Miles' road race.

They put me in a kennel hoping to find my owner.

My owner never came for me.

So this is where I lived for almost five years.

In the beginning I used to love to hang out with the other dogs and enjoy group activities.

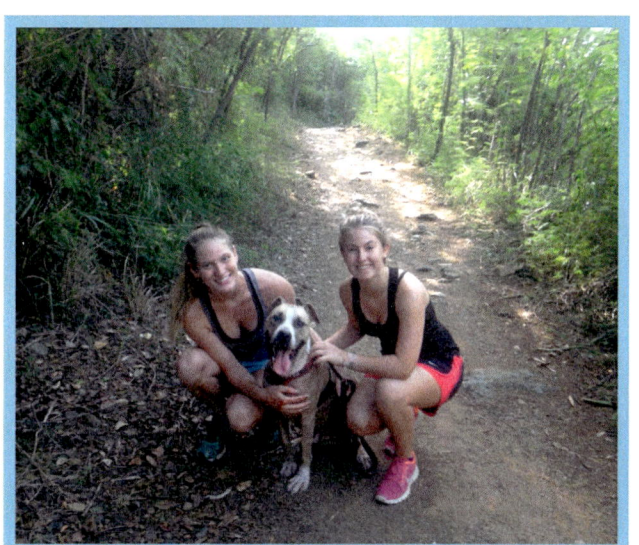

People on vacation would come in and take me for walks. They're called Voluntourists.

Rob, one of my favorite volunteers, would take me hiking every Sunday. Sundays were my favorite days.

In my first two years at the ACC, I really liked other dogs.

But living like this for so long, watching all my friends get adopted got to me and I started acting out. I took my frustrations out on other dogs, some of the cats at the feeding station at the ACC and even on the iguanas that I would see on my walks.

I then had to be kept away from the other dogs and animals. It made me sad, but it was best for all the other animals.

It also made it even harder to get me adopted.

So the volunteers started taking me out on fun outings.
This is my first ever selfie.

Missie always made me smile,
	and I always tried to do the same for her.

Ryan the Shelter Manager never played favorites,
but I think he had a special place in his heart for me.

In the nearly five years I spent at the shelter there were four different managers, and each one treated me like a King. No matter what; these four people always showed me love.

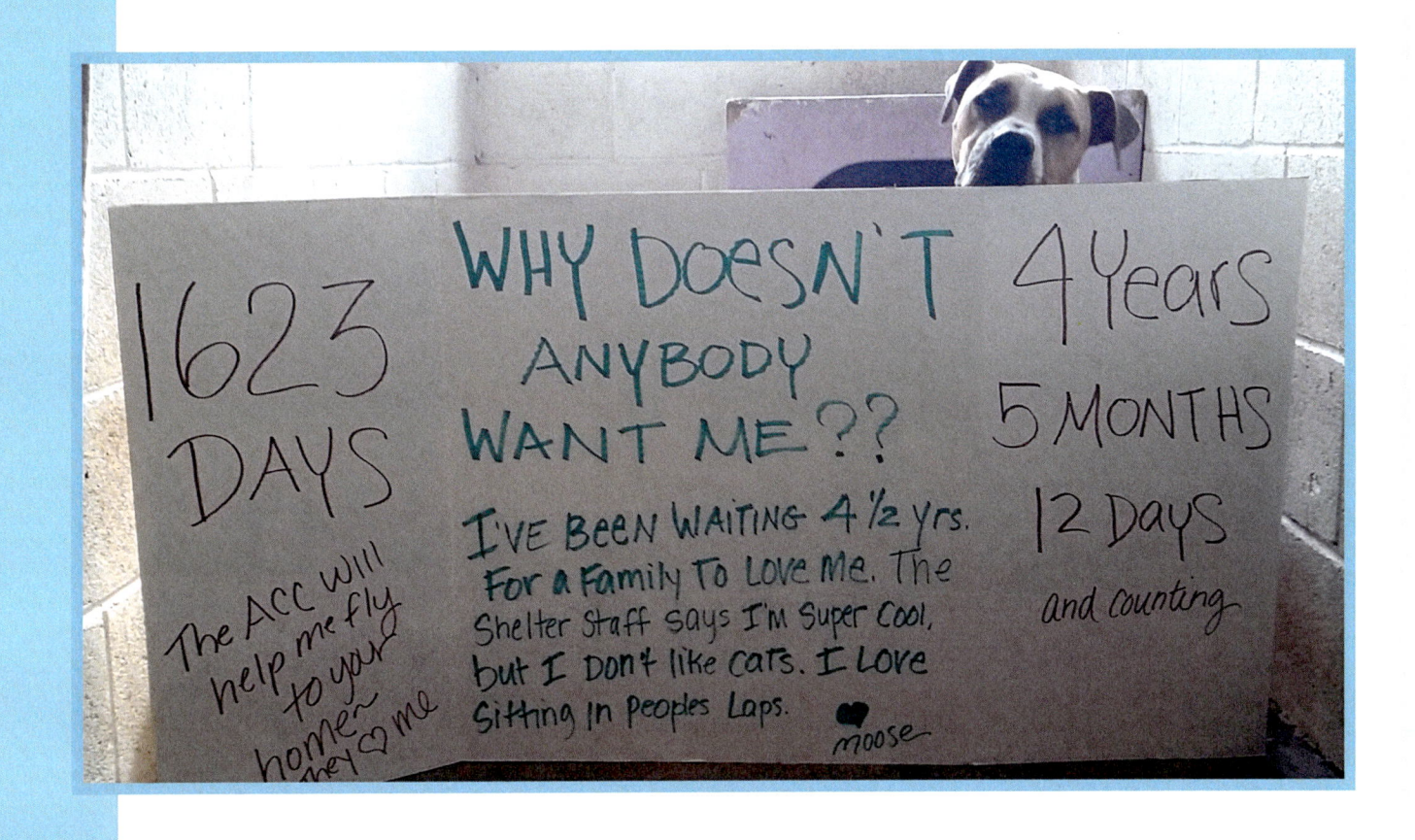

> **1623 DAYS**
> The ACC will help me fly to your home~ hey ♡ me
>
> **WHY DOESN'T ANYBODY WANT ME??**
> I'VE BEEN WAITING 4½ yrs. For a Family To Love Me. The Shelter Staff says I'm Super Cool, but I Don't like Cats. I Love Sitting In Peoples Laps. ♥ moose
>
> **4 Years**
> **5 MONTHS**
> **12 Days**
> and counting

Then one day a volunteer decided to make me my own Facebook page and posted this photo and I'm pretty sure that's when my life changed forever.

I became kinda famous...
My post was seen by over 300,000 people and was shared almost 4000 times. Suddenly thousands of people liked me and were networking to try and find me a home.

But everyone was still really nervous about how I would do in a home since I never had lived inside one before and I just didn't like cats. The shelter staff also wouldn't let me go to a home with other dogs in case I started to act out again.

So many people wanted me, but most already had pets.

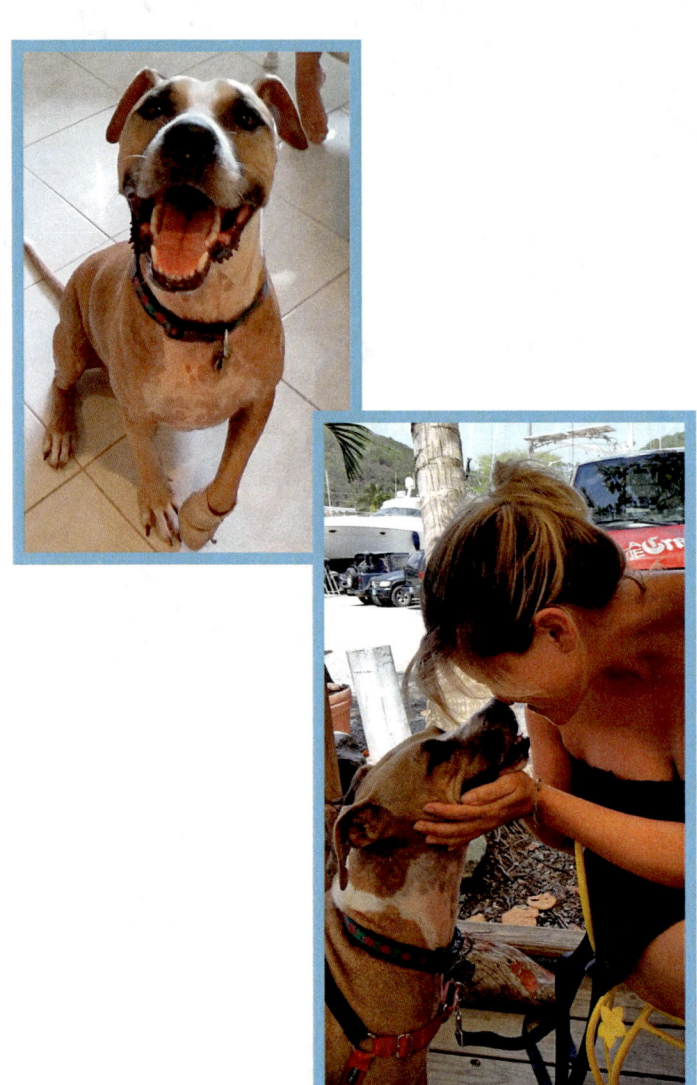

Then I met Mandi who lived on St Thomas and she decided to give me a chance and foster me to see how I could do in a home. I did my best and proved to everyone I am worthy of a home.

Mandi could not keep me forever. My foster time had to come to an end. It was hard to leave her, but she helped me show everyone that I was a good boy.

The Shelter staff needed a miracle for me.......

Where a last hope becomes a new beginning.

Then they heard about Last Hope K9 Rescue in Boston, Massachusetts.

They had followed 'The Story of Moose,' and offered to partner with the ACC to find me a home.

I was beyond grateful. With an organization like this, I was sure to find a family to love, a family I deserved. I now had two teams of amazing people working for me.

This is the awesome team from LHK9 who started working on my behalf. I call them Team Boston. They love me too.

To make me more adoptable, the ACC sent me for some training to Paradise Paws VI on St Thomas for a month. Lots of people donated to help pay for it... I am so grateful.

I love my Trainer, Paris. I learned to listen to all the commands he taught me.

Everyone knew I always had the skills, but they just didn't know how to bring them out. Paris helped prove I'm a good boy who just wants to please.

DEAR SANTA,

YOU KNOW WHAT I WANT.
I PROMISE I HAVE BEEN
A GOOD BOY.

PLEASE GIVE ME A FAMILY
FOR CHRISTMAS.

LOVE
MOOSE

My Christmas Wish

Then the Burke family in Massachusetts heard about my story. They recently lost their dog, Tasha and had not been ready to get another dog. When they saw my photo and read my story, they knew that we needed to be together.

So they contacted Last Hope K9 Rescue

I GOT ADOPTED!!!

Ok, where I'm going I gotta remember... 'Patriots, Bruins, Red Sox, Celtics. They're all wicked good'. I got this.

My first Christmas gift was a hoodie my family bought for me.

LHK9 did a really thorough job during my adoption process and said they were the perfect family for me.

The last step in my journey was to get me to Boston. My Team didn't think it was a good idea for me to fly under the plane. After almost 5 years in the shelter, they didn't want to do anything that might stress me out or affect me.

This is the Riggi family. Vincent and Patty Riggi were on St John for vacation with their family and heard about my plea for a ride.

They have huge hearts and spend a lot of time giving back and said they would be honored to fly me to my new home in their plane.

Vince and Patty are my heroes — they came and visited me a lot during their vacation.

I'm getting really good at posing for selfies. Nicole and I look good together.

Patty says I get to sit with her on the plane.

St John is called Love City for a good reason.

Before I left I was given a going away party so I could say good bye to some of my friends who love me.

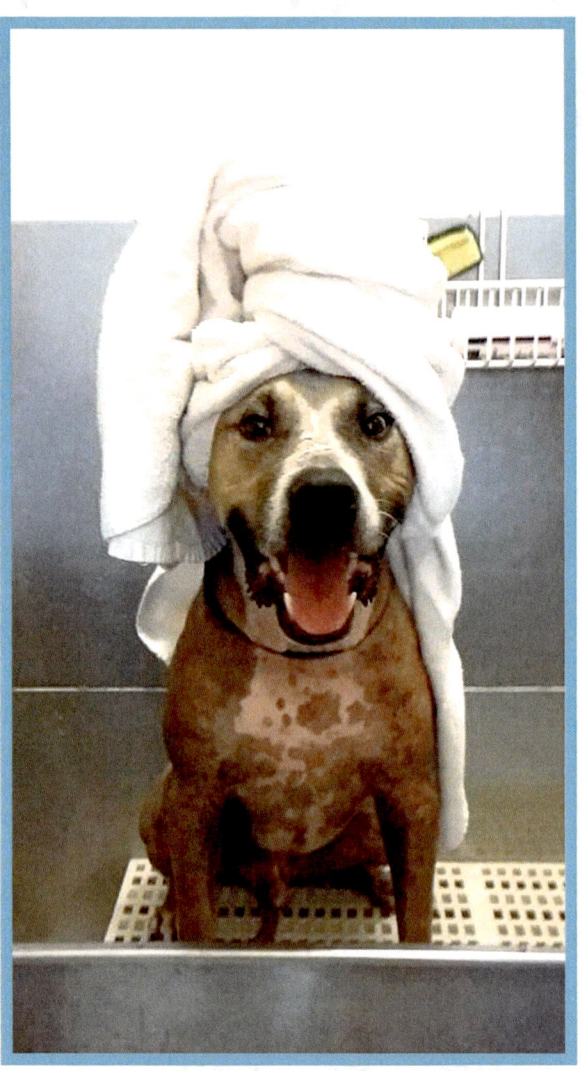

The day before I left I was treated to a Spa Day and lots of people stopped by to say good bye.

Laurie drove Ryan and me to the airport, and then I had to say good bye to her.

She was there the day I arrived at the shelter and she is one of the many people who never gave up on me and worked really hard at finding me a home. She tried not to let me see her tears, but I saw them and she saw mine.

Look at me getting ready to fly on a private jet. Do they know I'm just a shelter dog?

My adventure began...
there was a blizzard happening where we were going, but Vince and Patty told me not to worry.

Ryan relaxed when it hit him that this was really happening.

Patty let me have the sofa. I always cross my legs when I'm relaxing.

Bye-bye Virgin Islands,... and all my friends.

I loved all over the Riggi family on my flight so they would know how much they mean to me. Their hearts are huge.

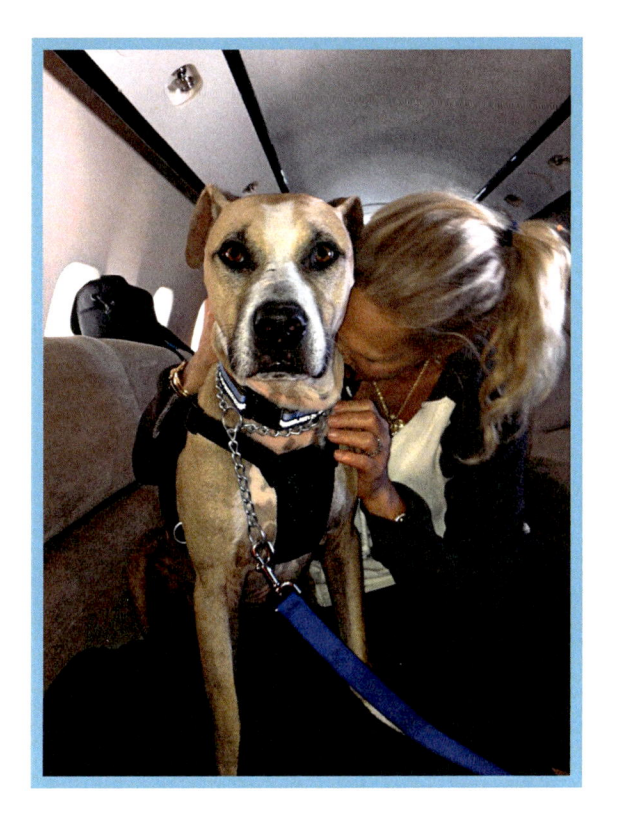

I arrived in the "States".

I said good bye to my angel Patty when we landed. I hope I get to see her again some day.

The door opened and WOW was it cold in Albany. Who knew!

These are my pilots Greg and William from XOJet. The were told about my story during the flight and they wanted to have their picture taken with me.

They heard I'm a celebrity.

This was the next leg of my journey. Vince and Patty got me and Ryan a limo to go to Boston from Albany. We don't have these in St John. I knew I wasn't in the islands anymore.

We drove into a blizzard on the way to Worcester Animal Rescue League. Because I am a shelter dog, I need to be quarantined for 48 hours.

When we were 10 minutes away we got stuck on some ice trying to get there. A good Samaritan stopped and helped us and then showed us a different way to go.

When we got to the Animal Rescue League my new family was there waiting for me. They drove over an hour through the blizzard just to meet me before I went into quarantine. I loved them the minute I saw them.

They gave me treats and hugs and then I had to be put in the quarantine suite for the next 2 days. All I kept thinking about was how nice they were and I hope I get to see them again.

But two days later they came back for me and we went home..... Everyone had a smile on their face; including me.

It was time to say good bye to Ryan. We've had quite a journey together. He kissed me and left quick. He's not so good with goodbyes. He's watched over me for years. I know I'll see him again; we will always be family.

I spent the day snuggling with my family. I've only known them for a short time, but WOW are they nice. And I'm pretty sure they love me.

What, little people in a box? And whoa — does it look cold. We don't ever see temps like that where I'm from!

My family keeps putting blankets on me. It feels so comfy. I've never imagined having a bed like this before.

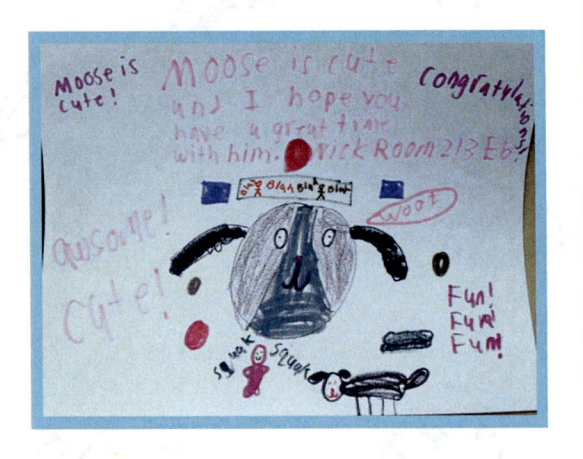

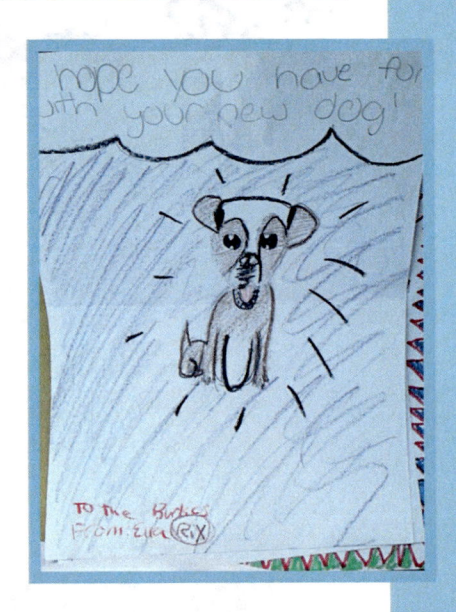

Miss Jenn, the third grade teacher at GWM middle school in East Bridgewater told her class about me and all about rescuing a shelter dog and her class wanted to make special cards for me. I am so lucky.

This is Christine and Bob. They took a chance on me and changed my life. I really love them.

I am Moose and I am home.

43

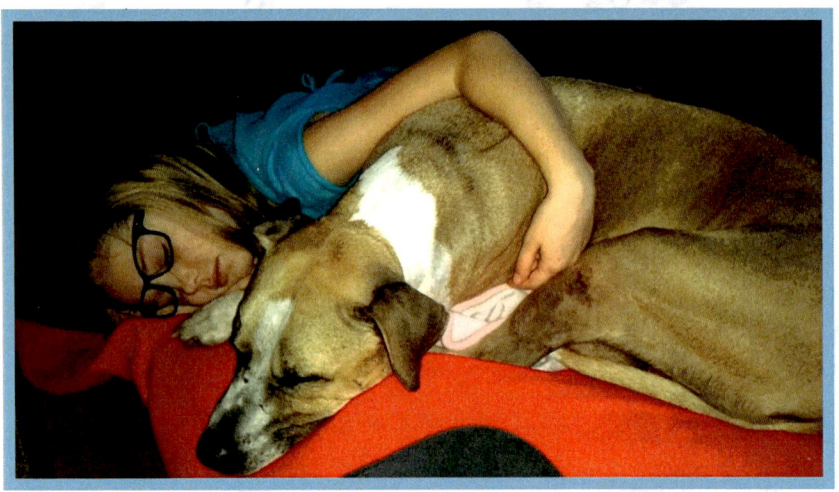

I have come to realize that this is where I live. This is my family.

I am Moose and I am loved.

Thank you to everyone who followed my story and rooted for me to find a home.

Thank you Animal Care Center of St John for loving me for almost 5 years and never giving up. I am grateful you are a no kill shelter and you gave me all the time I needed to find my family. Thank you Last Hope K9 Rescue in Boston for partnering with the ACC and finding my family.

Thank you Family for finding me and taking a chance. I'll love you forever.

I am Moose and I am not a shelter dog anymore.

Photos from my Scrapbook

A Message from Moose:

If you are considering a dog….please visit your local shelter. Look for the dogs that have been there a long time, or the senior dogs, or the very scared dogs or the dogs with medical issues….they need you.

If you can't adopt, please consider fostering.

If you can't foster, please consider volunteering.

Everyone can make a difference. All it takes it just one chance. Give them that chance. Volunteers changed my life. My foster got me ready for my new life, and my adopters are my life.

We can be good and we are worth it.

Made in the USA
Middletown, DE
18 March 2016